COMMUNICATION

YESTERDAY'S SCIENCE
TODAY'S TECHNOLOGY
SCIENCE ACTIVITIES

COMMUNICATION

ROBERT GARDNER

DRAWINGS BY DORIS ETTLINGER

TWENTY-FIRST CENTURY BOOKS

A DIVISION OF HENRY HOLT AND COMPANY / NEW YORK

Twenty-First Century Books
A Division of Henry Holt and Company, Inc.
115 West 18th Street
New York, NY 10011

Henry Holt® and colophon are trademarks of
Henry Holt and Company, Inc.
Publishers since 1866

Published in Canada by Fitzhenry & Whiteside Ltd.
195 Allstate Parkway, Markham, Ontario L3R 4T8

Library of Congress Cataloging-in-Publication Data
Gardner, Robert, 1929–
Communication / Robert Gardner.—1st ed.
p.   cm.—(Yesterday's Science, today's technology)
Includes index.
1. Communication and technology—Juvenile literature. [1. Communication—
Experiments. 2. Experiments.] I. Title. II. Series: Gardner, Robert, 1929–
Yesterday's science, today's technology.
P96.T42G37   1994
303.48'33—dc   94–21865
                                         CIP
                                         AC
First edition—1994
ISBN 0-8050-2854-4

Printed in the United States of America
All first editions printed on acid-free paper ∞.

1 3 5 7 9 10 8 6 4 2

Photo Credits

p. 14 (top and bottom): courtesy of Georgia Pacific Corp. ; p. 20: © North Wind Picture
Archives; p. 24: © Nicholas de Sciose/Photo Researchers, Inc.; p. 32: © The Bettmann
Archive; p. 47: © Sentrol, Inc.; pp. 64, 79: courtesy of AT&T Archives; p. 71: © Ida Mae
Astute/ABC

CONTENTS

Black-and-White TV/A Close Look at a Color TV
Screen/Magnetic Tape

4 COMMUNICATION IN THE FUTURE

A Light Pipe

INTRODUCTION

Carefully conducted experiments indicate that many animals, including bees, are able to communicate in one way or another. But the ability to communicate through words and in so many different ways are traits that distinguish humans from other forms of life. Early human communication may have been limited to grunts and gestures, but somewhere along the way we learned to speak—to make sounds that conveyed our thoughts, wants, and ideas to others.

Speech remains our most common way of communicating. Nevertheless, the fact that you call these bound pages *book* while Spaniards refer to it as *libro* reveals how different sounds may indicate the same thing. To most humans, the word *book* has no meaning. Only to the fraction of the world's population who speak English does *book* indicate the thing you now hold in your hands. Cultures without books, such as the Australian Aborigines, have no word for it.

By using symbols to indicate words, humans found a way to communicate without being within earshot of one another. But it was not until printing was developed that we could communicate our ideas to hundreds, thousands, and eventually millions of others. Printing provided a way for knowledge to spread rapidly across the world.

The invention of the telegraph in 1837 enabled people to communicate quickly with others who were far away. The telegraph was based on electrical technology that had been developed in the previous decade. Other inventions that allowed for almost immediate communication over long distances also depended on electrical technology. They include the telephone, wireless, radio, television, and fax machines.

In this book, you'll have an opportunity to investigate some of the science and technology associated with communication. You'll learn, through your reading and in a hands-on fashion, some of the basic principles that make communication possible. Each chapter contains a number of activities designed to enhance your understanding of the subject. You will find a ✖ beside a few activities. The ✖ indicates that you should ask an adult to help you because the activity may involve an action or the use of something that might be dangerous. Be sure to find adult help before attempting activities marked in this way.

Other activities, preceded by a ★, might serve as starting points for a science-fair project. Bear in mind, however, that judges at such contests are looking for original ideas and creative thinking. Projects copied from a book are not likely to impress anyone. However, you may find that one or more of the activities in this book will stimulate a project or experiment of your own design that will lead you to the winner's circle at your school's next science or invention fair.

1

COMMUNICATING THROUGH WRITING: THE PRINTED WORD

Today's electronic printing methods are based on engineering and the science of electricity that led to electronics, lasers, and computers. In fact, the book you are reading was written on a computer—a tool that has been as big a boon to writing as the pencil. But the technology of printing was established through the work of craftsmen. It was not based on scientific principles. However, the growth of science itself, because it is so dependent on the repetition of experiments by critics, could never have blossomed without printing, books, and journals.

Writing enabled humans to communicate thoughts, feelings, and ideas without being present. It extended communication to people far away, provided that written words could be transported over such distances. Through writing, ideas could be transmitted from generation to generation without distortion, as so often happens with spoken language. It was through written records that Western civilization became aware of the magnificent culture of ancient Greece. The most important impact of writing, however, may have been in commerce and government. Written records of business transactions, laws, and regulations reduced the debates over what was actually said and meant when an agreement was signed or a law enacted. You probably know through experience how difficult it is for people to agree on what was actually said a week or even a day ago. The following activity may help you to understand why.

A C T I V I T Y I

WHAT'S LOST IN TRANSMITTING SPOKEN WORDS?

MATERIALS
- *a dozen or more people*
- *two written messages*
- *paper and pencils*

For this activity, you'll need a number of people—a dozen or more if possible—so it might be done at a party or a family gathering. You'll need two written messages that you should prepare ahead of time. One might be the following:

> *A coming storm, your shooting corns presage,*
> *And aches will throb; your hollow tooth will rage.*

You may prefer to write something of your own. If you do, make it short enough so it can be remembered but long enough so the listener has to concentrate. Avoid common sayings, poems, or slogans that everyone knows.

Ask the people to sit in a row. Whisper the words you have written to the first person in the row. That person will then whisper what he or she heard to the next person and so on until the last person receives the message. Ask each person to record on a sheet of paper what he or she heard. How does the message recorded by the last person in the row compare with the original words that you whispered? What changes appear as the message moves from one person to the next?

Repeat the experiment, but this time pass a sheet of paper that has another written message along the row of people. It might be another old-weather saying such as:

> *To talk of the weather is nothing but folly;*
> *When it rains on the hill, the sun's in the valley.*

After everyone has read the message, ask each of them to write what they read on the paper. How does their ability to record a written message correctly compare with their ability to record a message passed from person to person by word of mouth?

Paper and Writing

Early records and writings were done on clay tablets, but by 2000 B.C. Egyptians were writing on parchment—dried sheep or goat skin. There were no pencils or pens. Lines were scratched on the parchment with a sharp stick, stone, or reed. Later, they used papyrus made by weaving together fibers peeled from reeds. The fibers were coated with gum (sized) to provide a smooth surface that could be written on with an inked brush.

In the first century, the Chinese were making paper to replace the silk, bamboo, and wooden tablets that had been used to write on. They mixed fibrous hemp and ramie plants with rattan and mulberry, which was then finely chopped before being boiled with wood ashes. After washing, the liquid pulp was poured on porous screens, where it dried.

It was another 1,000 years before paper mills were established in Europe. In these mills, linen rags, sometimes mixed with cotton and straw, were used to make pulp. By the sixteenth century, Europeans were sizing (adding fillers to hold the fibers together) the dried, very absorbent paper sheets to reduce smudging.

A MAGNIFIED VIEW OF PAPER

MATERIALS
- *different kinds of paper*
- *strong magnifying glass or microscope*
- *water*
- *food coloring*
- *drinking glass*
- *eyedropper*
- *window or lamp*

Use a strong magnifying glass or the low-power lenses of a microscope to examine various kinds of paper. Make a small tear in the paper to see the fibers more clearly. Examine different kinds of paper—writing, computer, towels, wrapping, facial and bathroom tissues, and so on. What differences do you see in the fibers found in these various kinds of paper?

Place a drop of water to which food coloring has been added near the torn edge of each of the sheets you examined. With a magnifying glass, watch the way water enters the paper. Does the rate at which water travels into the paper depend on the kind of paper being tested? If it does, can you explain why?

Hold the various kinds of paper up to the light from a window or lamp. How do the papers differ in their ability to transmit light? Can you explain why?

MAKING PAPER

MATERIALS

- *stiff wire window screen*
- *tin shears*
- *large aluminum frozen-food container*
- *an old curtain*
- *basin, such as a dishpan, large enough to hold the aluminum pan and 10 L (2½ gal) of water*
- *facial tissue (not "wet strength")*
- *warm water*
- *blender (optional)*
- *tablespoon for stirring and measuring*
- *instant laundry starch*
- *eggbeater*
- *newspaper or blotter paper*
- *rolling pin*
- *electric household iron*
- *scissors*

Large papermaking machines produce as much as 100 tons of paper per day. Early craftsmen might make 500 sheets in a day. Despite changes in production rate, the ingredients and processes are quite similar. Wood or cotton fibers are mixed with water to form a suspension. The suspension is poured onto fine mesh screens so water can drain from the fibers. The wet fibrous mat is then squeezed and heated to remove any remaining water.

To make your own paper, begin by preparing the screen onto which the pulp will be poured and its container. Use tin shears to trim a piece of stiff window screen to fit the bottom of a large aluminum frozen-food container. Cover the screen

Large wood chippers are used in the first stage of papermaking.

Paper can be made in various weights, sizes, colors, and finishes. A modern papermaking machine can produce 100 tons of paper in one day.

with a piece of old curtain. (If you have only soft, flexible screening, build a wooden frame to fit inside the container, stretch the screen across the frame, and hold it in place with thumbtacks.) Use the shears to cut out the bottom of the aluminum pan, leaving a 2-cm (¾-in.) lip to support the screen, as shown in Figure 1a. Then find a basin, such as a dishpan, that is large enough to hold the aluminum pan and 10 L (2½ gal) of water.

Now comes the chemistry. Since you probably don't have fine wood fibers, which have to be separated from small wood chips and then bleached, you can tear about 30 sheets of facial tissue into pieces about 2.5 cm (1 in.) on a side. (Don't use "wet strength" tissues!) Drop the torn tissues into the basin, add 1.4 L (1½ quarts) of warm water, and stir for 10 to 15 minutes to make a pulp. If you'd like, ask an adult to make the pulp in a blender.

To prepare the size, add one tablespoon of instant laundry starch to two cups of warm water and stir. Mix the size and pulp together in the basin. Add 4 L (1 gal) more of warm water and beat with an eggbeater until the fibers are spread thoroughly and uniformly throughout the mixture.

Place an opened newspaper several sheets thick or a sheet of blotter paper on a table or the floor. Then, holding the screen firmly against the lip of the aluminum pan, dip it into the pulpy mixture in the basin as shown in Figure 1b. Turn the pan so it is horizontal and lift it from the basin. A thin layer of pulp should remain on top of the screen. Allow the water to drain away as you gently shake the screen and pan.

Gripping opposite edges of the screen, lift it from the pan. Place the pulp-covered screen on the paper. Close the newspaper (or cover the pulp with a second sheet of blotter paper) and carefully turn it over so that the screen is now on top of the pulp. Use a rolling pin to squeeze water from the pulp. The newspaper or blotter paper above and below the pulp will absorb the water.

a.

screen

3/4" lip on bottom of pan

large aluminum frozen-food pan

rest of bottom cut away

b.

screen & curtain resting on lip of pan

aluminum pan

pulp

basin

newspaper or blotter

Figure 1. Making paper the old-fashioned way!

Finally, ask an adult to help you use an electric household iron (set on warm, not hot) to press-dry the sheet between the newspaper or blotter sheets. After the pulp is thoroughly dry, you may remove it from the screen and trim it to a desired size with the scissors.

Can you write on the paper you have made? How is the paper different from the paper you normally write on? Why do you think it's different?

Repeat the experiment without adding starch to the pulp. Do you see any difference between paper made with and without starch? If the paper you've made is too thick or too thin, what can you do to obtain the proper thickness?

Early Printing

Again, it was the Chinese who first developed printing. Their first "printing presses" were made by incising characters on a smooth slab of stone. Moist paper was then spread on the slab and worked into the incisions. After the paper had dried, it was wiped with an inked pad. Because ink did not enter the depressions, the final copy had white characters on a dark background, giving a negative print (see Figure 2). The process was slow, but, other than copying by hand or using a seal, it was probably the first method used to make multiple copies of a document.

Later, positive printing was done by placing a handwritten inked sheet facedown on a wooden slab. The wood was then carved away, leaving elevated characters on the slab. After the characters were covered with ink, a sheet of paper was pressed against them to make a copy. This could be repeated thousands of times.

Movable type appeared first in China during the eleventh century. The characters, made of clay, were heated to make them hard. A shallow iron tray covered with a soft mixture of wax, resin, and ash served as a base for holding the characters, which were then inked before paper was pressed onto them. With a large num-

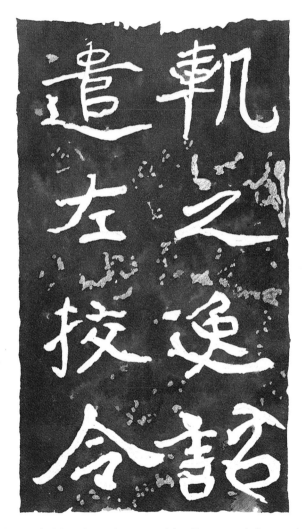

Figure 2. Negative print, something like an artist's negative space, was the result of incising characters into a smooth slab of stone. Wet paper placed on the stone was worked into the incisions. When coated with ink, only the depressed characters remained white.

ber of characters available, a printer could readily prepare a tray for printing.

Johannes Gutenberg (c. 1400–1468) established the first printing press in Europe at Mainz, Germany, in about 1445. His press showed a definite Chinese influence, but his characters were made from a tin-based alloy and he used an oil-based ink. The characters were set in a chase (a frame), held in place with wedges, and inked. A sheet of paper was attached to a frame (tympan) connected to the chase by hinges. The paper was often large enough to print 8 pages at a time (16 when both sides were used). The tympan and chase were slid under a flat plate (platen) used to press the paper against the print. A large screw, turned by a lever, was used to apply force to the platen. To even out any variation in pressure due to small differences in the height of the print, the tympan was lined with a sheet of felt.

Printing in China developed slowly, even though it was invented there, because a printer had to use thousands of different characters to set print. In Europe, using an alphabet, printing revolutionized communication. A printer needed only about 50 different characters (including the letters of the alphabet). Within 50 years after Gutenberg's first publication, more than 40,000 works totaling some 20 million copies had been printed.

Modern Methods of Printing

The three most common methods of printing today are letterpress, gravure, and lithography. As you can see from Figure 3a, the plate used in letterpress has raised characters. Ink applied to the letters is transferred to paper when the paper is pressed against them. In present-day letterpress printers, the type is set mechanically as directed from a keyboard outside the press itself.

In gravure or intaglio printing (see Figure 3b), the process is similar except that the characters exist as depressions in the plate. Before paper is pressed against the plate, a so-called doctor blade sweeps across the surface, clearing away ink between the characters.

Gutenberg's printing press

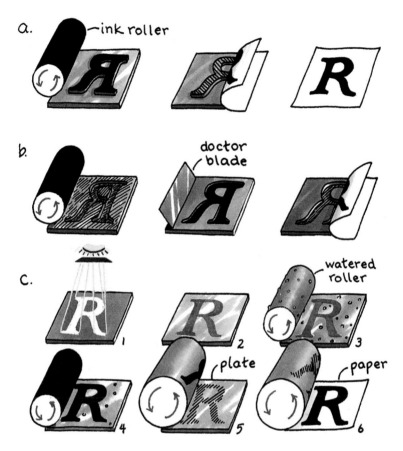

a. ink roller

b. doctor blade

c. watered roller

plate

paper

Figure 3: a. In letterpress, ink is applied to raised characters on a plate. When paper is pressed against the plate, ink is transferred to the paper. b. In gravure, the characters are engraved. After inking, a doctor blade removes ink from the flat portions of the plate before paper is pressed against the plate and the ink transferred from the characters to the paper. c. In lithography (1) A photo is projected onto a lithographic plate. (2) The plate is treated with a greasy material that sticks to the dark parts of the image. (3) The plate is wetted. (4) The plate is inked. The ink sticks to the greasy parts of the plate but not the wetted parts. (5) The inked image is transferred to a rubber-coated cylinder. (6) The rubberized cylinder transfers the ink to paper.

In lithography, or photo-offset printing (see Figure 3c), the original page is photographed. The photograph is then projected onto a lithographic plate—a thin sheet of zinc or aluminum that has a special chemical coating. During development, a greasy material is deposited on the plate in the dark parts of the image that are to take on ink. The rest of the plate remains clean and shiny. A drum carrying the plate is wetted by a watered roller before a separate inked roller moves over the plate. The water is repelled by greasy portions of the plate but remains on the shiny parts. The ink, in turn, is repelled by the wet areas but sticks to the grease. The inked image is transferred from the plate to a rubber-coated cylinder that applies the ink to paper.

Many books today are set into print by means of a laser typesetter. A keyboard used to prepare the text sends signals to a typesetter and a laser beam illuminates the film. The computer turns the laser on and off as it moves across the film. When the film is developed, the images created by laser light appear as text. The film can then be projected onto plates coated with light-sensitive chemicals. Further treatment of the plates depends on which method of printing will be used.

Obviously, the use of laser-beam technology was impossible before Theo Maiman (1927–   ) invented the ruby laser in 1960. Here, then, is another example of a technology based on a scientific development—a development that many believed had no practical value.

 ACTIVITY 4

A SIMPLE LETTERPRESS PRINTER

MATERIALS
- *flat toothpicks*
- *sharp knife*
- *two small flat boards about 8 cm (3 in.) on a side*

- *glue*
- *ink or ink pad*
- *white paper*

To make a simple letterpress printer, ask an adult to help you cut some flat toothpicks into small pieces. You can assemble the pieces to make letters that spell out a word, such as *end*. The letters can then be glued to a flat board. But remember, in letterpress printing, paper will be pressed against the inked letters on the board to produce a printed page. Should the letters be upside down or right side up? Should they be written forward or backward? Should they start on the right or the left side of the board?

Once you have decided how the letters and the word should be arranged, glue the letters onto a flat board and let the glue dry thoroughly. You can then apply ink to the letters with an ink pad or a small brush, such as a watercolor brush, that has been dipped in ink. Hold the paper firmly against the second board and press the paper firmly against the raised letters on the first board. Turn the paper over and look at the printed word. Did you arrange the letters in the word correctly? If not, what changes must you make to obtain a correctly printed word?

Colored Print

Printing a book with colored diagrams or pictures requires only four inks—black, cyan (bluish green), yellow, and magenta. But separate plates are prepared for each ink. Colored portions of each sheet are scanned to determine the amount of each color in each portion of the plate. The black plate is made from a black-and-white image of the diagram or picture. A computer uses the light signals from the scanner to produce dots of different sizes for each of the four plates. Large dots closely spaced indicate intense light; small dots far apart indicate weak light.

This huge press can print six colors at one time.

When the sheets are printed, they pass through each of four separate inked plates, one for each color. As shown in Figure 4, the four inks are applied separately in dotlike fashion according to information that was recorded by the computer in response to the scanner as it analyzed for black and the three colors. For example, the green portion of a colored photograph will receive dots of cyan ink and yellow ink. The combination of these two inks will be seen as green by a reader. Similarly, blue parts of the photo will receive dots of cyan and magenta ink; red parts will be covered with dots of yellow and magenta ink.

The next activity will help you to see how a mix of colors can produce other colors. The last two activities in this chapter will include a view of the tiny dots used in printing colors and the way a 16-page layout is folded after printing to produce pages properly ordered by number.

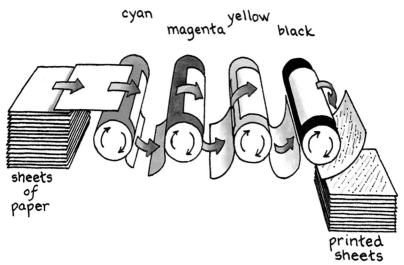

cyan magenta yellow black

sheets of paper

printed sheets

Figure 4. Color printing is done from four separate plates by using cyan, magenta, yellow, and black inks.

PRINT AND THE ADDITION
AND SUBTRACTION OF COLOR

MATERIALS
- *blue, green, and red lightbulbs and lamps, preferably study lamps with cone-shaped metallic shades*
- *dark room*
- *white screen or wall*
- *watercolors and brush*
- *water*
- *white paper*
- *strong light*

All the colors in the rainbow can be made by adding red, green, and blue light to one another. To see this for yourself, shine light from blue, green, and red lightbulbs on a white screen or wall in a dark room. If the bulbs are in study lamps, the colored lights can be directed quite well. Overlapping beams of blue and red light produce a color called magenta. Blue and green light combine to produce a bluish green color—cyan. What color do you see when red light is added to green light?

You can produce white light by mixing all three colored lights. Results may improve if you move one lamp closer and another farther from the wall or screen.

Colored pigments in filters, cloth, paints, or liquids subtract colors from a beam of white light. For example, a good red filter will remove every color but red. Similarly, a blue filter will subtract all but blue from a white light beam; green filters absorb all colors except green.

To see how pigments subtract colors, you'll need a set of watercolors and a small brush, water, and white paper. See if you can identify cyan, magenta, and yellow paints in the set of watercolors. Some sets have colors that are very nearly pure blue, red, and green. When two of these colors are mixed, they produce a very dark mixture because they reflect very little light. Figure 5 shows how different pigments reflect and absorb the colors found in white light.

If you can identify cyan, magenta, and yellow pigments, use the brush to mix cyan and magenta pigments on a sheet of white paper. You will find that you can produce a deep blue color. Cyan pigments reflect blue and green light and absorb red light. Magenta pigments absorb green light and reflect blue and red light. Since blue is the only color reflected by both cyan and magenta pigments, a mixture of the two will appear blue.

A mixture of magenta and yellow paints in the proper proportion will appear red because red is the only colored light reflected by both pigments. Yellow pigments absorb blue light and magenta pigments absorb green light.

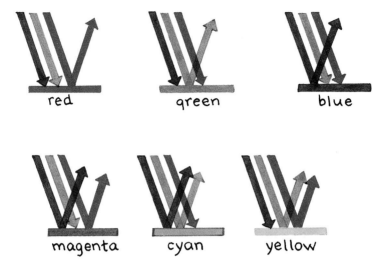

Figure 5. White light, a mixture of red, green, and blue light, is shown here shining on six different pigments—red, green, blue, yellow, magenta, and cyan. What parts of the white light are reflected by each of the pigments?

What color do you expect to see if you mix cyan and yellow paints on white paper? Try it! Was your prediction correct?

Cyan and red light are said to be complementary because the combination of red and cyan light will produce white light. Remember, cyan is a combination of green and blue light. For the same reason, magenta and green are complementary colors. What would be the complementary color of blue light?

COLORED DOTS, NEWSPAPERS, MAGAZINES, AND BOOKS

MATERIALS
- *strong magnifying glass*
- *black-and-white and colored diagrams or photographs from books, magazines, or newspapers*

Use a strong magnifying glass to look at a black-and-white photograph in a newspaper, book, or magazine. How are different shades of gray produced in the printing process?

Now use the magnifier to look at some color pictures or drawings from similar sources. How are the colors produced? What is done to change the intensity of a color? Do you ever find other colored dots in a portion of a photograph that appears to be uniformly blue, yellow, green, or some other color? Can you identify which parts of the photo or drawing were on one or more of the original plates used in the printing process? Do you ever find color so intense that you can't identify the individual dots?

Compare the sizes of the colored dots found in different types of print—newspapers, books, expensive glossy magazines. How is dot size related to the quality of the picture?

SIXTEEN PAGES ON ONE SHEET

MATERIALS
- *sheet of paper*
- *ruler*
- *pencil*
- *scissors*

Printing presses usually print 16 pages on a single large sheet. To see how this can be done, use a ruler to divide a sheet of paper into eight equal areas on each side, as shown in Figure 6. Figure 6 also shows you how to number each of the areas so that when you fold the sheet properly these will be the num-

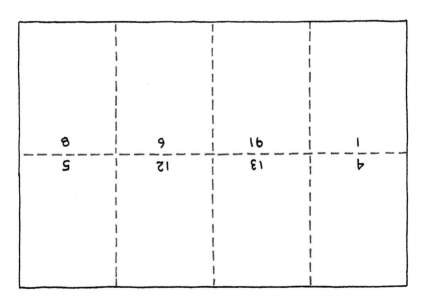

Figure 6. This sheet when numbered on the back, folded, and properly cut constitutes a 16-page signature. The signature would then be bound, quite likely with other signatures, to make a book.

bers in proper sequence on separate pages. How will you number the areas on the other side of the sheet so that after you fold the sheet three times and make three cuts with scissors you will have 16 pages numbered in order from 1 to 16?

Binding Books

The 16 pages assembled in Activity 7 constitute a signature. A book usually contains one or more signatures. Are all the pages in a book numbered? What total number of pages might be commonly found in books? How many pages are in this book? How many signatures?

In putting a hardcover book together, the signatures are arranged in proper order and their backs are sewn together and glued. A lining is glued to the back and a cover is glued to stiffeners called boards and to the lining. Early books were bound by hand; today, the binding is done by machine.

What is used to bind most magazines?

2

COMMUNICATION BY WIRE

Printing spread ideas across the globe, but printed words could travel no faster than the mode of transportation (mostly boats) that carried them. The telegraph, patented in 1838, provided a means of almost-immediate communication in spite of distance. Later, in 1876, Alexander Graham Bell (1847–1922) uttered the famous words: "Mr. Watson, come here. I want you!" This event marked the introduction of long-distance communication by voice.

Both the telegraph and the telephone carry information by wire, and both are based on the principles of electricity and magnetism established by Hans Christian Oersted (1777–1851) early in the nineteenth century. The telegraph illustrates how quickly scientific discoveries are sometimes put to practical use. The technology associated with telegraphy was developed within two decades of Oersted's discovery.

The Telegraph

Hans Christian Oersted discovered the connection between electricity and magnetism in 1819. This led to the invention of the electromagnet by William Sturgeon (1783–1850) in 1823. By 1837, William Cooke (1806–1879) and Charles Wheatstone (1802–1875) had patented the telegraph, and a year later Samuel F. B. Morse (1791–1872) developed a code made of dots and dashes that could be used to transmit messages.

In 1844, Morse sent the first message ("What hath God wrought!") over a long-distance telegraph line between Washington, D.C., and Baltimore. About 15 years later, a 3,000 km (1,850-mi) transatlantic submarine cable was laid along the ocean floor by a huge former passenger ship, the *Great Eastern*. The cable allowed messages to be transmitted across the Atlantic Ocean, making possible almost-instant communication between the United States and Europe. Morse code was used extensively in World War II, but modern developments such as facsimile and printing telegraph machines have largely replaced Morse code.

An early receiver designed for the navy

BUILDING A TELEGRAPH SENDER AND RECEIVER

MATERIALS

- *sandpaper*
- *nail about 8 cm (3 in.) long*
- *about 3 m (10 ft) of #20 to #26 insulated (enameled) copper wire*
- *a dozen or so paper clips*
- *piece of soft wood about 9 cm (3.5 in.) by 15 cm (6 in.) by 2.5 cm (1 in.)*
- *another piece of soft wood about 9 cm (3.5 in.) by 8 cm (3 in.) by 1.3 cm (½ in.)*
- *a third piece of soft wood about 5 cm (2 in.) by 10 cm (4 in.) by 1.3 cm (½ in.)*
- *tape*
- *hammer*
- *cardboard strip 4 cm (1½ in.) by 8.5 cm (3.25 in.)*
- *5 unpainted metallic thumbtacks*
- *pliers*

Ask an adult to help you cut the pieces of wood you will need for this experiment. Then make the electromagnet that will be part of the telegraph sounder (receiver). As you may know, a coil of wire carrying an electric current behaves like a magnet.

At a point about 30 cm (1 ft) from one end of the 3 m (10 ft) of insulated wire, begin winding the wire around the large nail. Don't cover the last 2 cm (¾ in.) of the nail above its pointed tip. This part of the nail will be driven into a board later. Keep winding the wire, layer after layer, always in the same direction until about 30 cm (1 ft) of wire remains. Wrap the coiled wire with tape to hold it in place.

Use sandpaper to remove the insulation from the last inch of each end of the wire. Attach one of the ends to one pole of the 6-volt battery. When you touch the other end of the wire to the other pole of the battery, electric current will flow through the wire that surrounds the nail. (**Don't allow current to flow for long. You'll wear down the battery if you do.**) Hold the wire to the battery as you bring the head of the nail near some paper clips, as shown in Figure 7. What happens? How can you tell that the nail is acting like a magnet? What happens when you break the circuit (remove the wire from the battery pole)? Will the electromagnet lift thumbtacks, as well?

To complete the construction of the telegraph, use small

Figure 7. An electromagnet made with insulated wire, a nail, and a battery will attract many metallic materials.

nails or glue to fasten the 9 cm (3.5 in.) by 8 cm (3 in.) by 1.3 cm (½ in.) board to one end of the larger piece of wood, as shown in Figure 8a. Hammer the nail into the larger piece of wood, being careful not to damage the wire. The head of the nail should be about 6.3 cm (2½ in.) from the upright piece of wood you just fastened and about 6 mm (¼ in.) lower than the top of that piece of wood. Fasten the foot-long ends of the wire to the board with thumbtacks, as shown in Figure 8a.

Push another thumbtack through the cardboard strip about 6 mm (¼ in.) from one end. Use pliers to bend the sharp end of the thumbtack down onto the cardboard so that it will remain in place when the cardboard strip is turned over. Fasten the other end of the cardboard to the upright piece of wood, as shown in Figure 8a. The head of the thumbtack over the nail should be on the bottom of the cardboard, about 6 mm (¼ in.) above the head of the nail.

Now build the sender, or switch, as shown in Figure 8b. Remove about an inch of insulation from each end of a 15 cm (6 in.) length of wire. Connect one end of the wire to one pole of the 6-volt dry-cell battery. Wrap the other end around a thumbtack and push it into the wood near one end of the 5 cm (2 in.) by 10 cm (4 in.) board. Use sandpaper to rough up the top of the thumbtack.

Open a paper clip as shown in Figure 8b. Wrap the end of one of the wires from the sounder to the smaller loop of the paper clip. Fasten this loop of the paper clip and the end of the wire to the 5 cm (2 in.) by 10 cm (4 in.) board with two thumbtacks. Leave the larger loop of the paper clip standing at a slight upward angle (as shown) over the first thumbtack you placed in the board.

To close the switch, push the large loop of the paper clip down onto the head of the thumbtack. There should be enough spring in the loop so that it will come back up off the thumbtack when you release it.

Finally, connect the second wire from the sounder to the other pole of the battery. Your telegraph is now ready for operation. To send a signal, briefly close the switch. When you do, the thumbtack on the cardboard will be attracted to the head of the nail and will make a click when it strikes. Open the switch by releasing the paper-clip loop and the thumbtack will spring back up.

If you close the switch only briefly, it creates a sound that corresponds to a dot in Morse code. Closing the switch for a slightly longer time produces a dash. Try making up your own

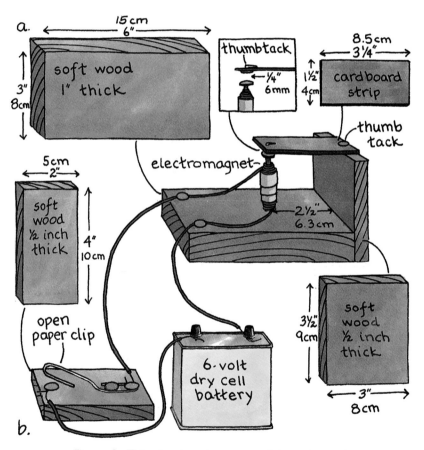

Figure 8. This drawing shows a. a telegraph receiver or sounder and b. a sender or switch.

code that you and a friend can share and send some messages using your telegraph.

With three long pieces of wire, you can set up a sender and receiver in different rooms, as shown in Figure 9. Then you and a friend can send messages back and forth between the rooms. How does the wiring shown in the drawing allow the sender in one room to activate the receiver in the other?

The Telephone

Although modern telephone systems require complex circuits, fiber optics, and communication satellites, the basic technology used to convert sounds to electrical signals in the sender and back to sound in the receiver is similar to that found in early telephones invented by Bell and modified by Thomas Edison (1847–1931).

When you speak, your vocal cords vibrate. These vibrations are transmitted by the air as sound waves—the back-and-forth motion of the air molecules that lie between speaker and listener. Figure 10 shows sound waves produced by a tuning fork. As the vibrating tines of the fork move back and forth, they alternately push air molecules together and then increase the distance between them. The compressed and expanded segments of air moving away from the tuning fork constitute the sound waves.

You can communicate by shouting if your listener is not far away, but sound waves spread out in all directions. The changes in pressure quickly become so small that they have no effect on the listener's eardrums and communication ceases. Bell was well aware of this. In fact, his invention stemmed from his interest in helping people who were deaf. He also realized that electric current follows a wire. It does not spread out and diminish rapidly like sound waves. This led him to search for a way to convert the energy in sound to electrical impulses.

Sound waves striking a flexible object such as the diaphragm in the mouthpiece of a telephone cause it to vibrate at the same

Figure 9. Notice that the wires in this telegraph system for sending "long-distance" messages allow the sender in room A to activate the sounder (receiver) in room B and vice versa. At P_1 and P_2, the insulation on the wires connecting switch and sounder must be removed so that wire W can be connected at these two points.

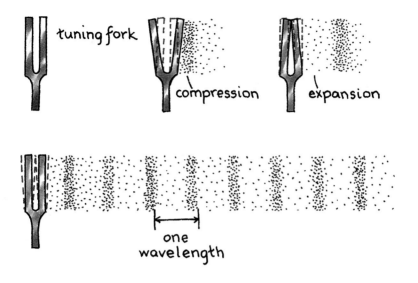

tuning fork

compression expansion

one
wavelength

Figure 10: a. A tuning fork alternately squeezes (compresses) molecules together and increases (expands) the distance between them. b. The continual vibration of the tuning fork produces a series of equally spaced compressions and expansions that spread outward. Together, these make up a sound wave. The distance between one compression (or expansion) and the next is one wavelength.

frequency as the sound waves. The diaphragm moves in with each compression and outward with each expansion of the wave. Behind the diaphragm, as you can see in Figure 11, are tiny black granules of carbon.

Edison discovered that the electrical resistance of carbon particles—the resistance of an electrical conductor to the flow of charge—changes with pressure. When resistance is high, relatively few charges flow per second; the electric current is small. When the resistance is low, more charges per second flow by any given point in the conductor.

As the diaphragm in a telephone mouthpiece vibrates, the pressure on the carbon granules behind it changes with each vibration and so does the electrical resistance and the current. As the resistance increases, the electric current decreases and vice versa. The

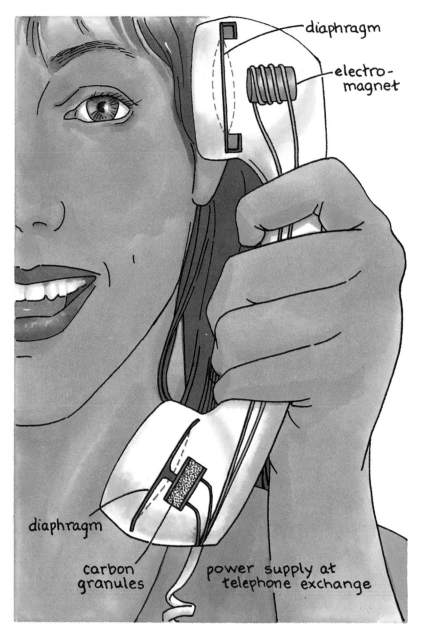

diaphragm

electro-magnet

diaphragm

carbon granules

power supply at telephone exchange

Figure 11. A telephone mouthpiece converts sound to electrical impulses. A telephone earpiece uses an electromagnet and diaphragm to convert electrical signals into sound.

electric current, therefore, varies in the same way as the air pressure in the sound wave. The changing electric current is carried by wires to an electromagnet in the receiver's earpiece.

When current in the electromagnet increases, the magnetic field in the electromagnet's iron core increases, too. As the current grows, the core, which acts like a magnet, attracts the thin metal diaphragm in the earpiece, causing it to move inward. When the current decreases, the diaphragm moves back.

The motion of the diaphragm depends on the current in the electromagnet, which, in turn, depends on the pressure from sound waves entering the mouthpiece. Consequently, the vibrations of the diaphragm in the earpiece duplicate those in the mouthpiece, although they are less intense.

ACTIVITY 9

TRANSMITTING SOUND WAVES

MATERIALS
- *balloon*
- *radio*
- *scissors*
- *can, such as a frozen-juice can, open at both ends*
- *rubber band, if necessary*
- *salt*

Blow up a balloon. Hold it with your fingertips as you bring it close to the speaker of a loud radio. Can you feel the balloon vibrating as sound waves from the radio strike it? How can you be sure it is sound from the radio that makes the balloon vibrate?

Hold the balloon in front of your mouth as you sing or talk. Can you feel the balloon vibrate in response to your voice?

Use scissors to cut the neck off a deflated balloon. Stretch the balloon over one end of a can from which both the top and bottom have been removed. (You may need a rubber band to hold the balloon firmly in place like the head of a drum.) Then sprinkle a few salt crystals on the surface of the balloon and hold it above a loud radio. What happens to the salt crystals? Can you explain why?

★ **ACTIVITY 10**

ELECTRIC CURRENT AND PRESSURE

MATERIALS
- *small magnetic compass*
- *4.5 m (5 yd) of #22, #24, or #26 enameled copper wire*
- *masking tape*
- *sandpaper*
- *clay*
- *D-cell*
- *graphite (you can buy tubes of graphite lubricant wherever hardware or auto supplies are sold)*
- *roofing nail*
- *old soup spoon*
- *insulated wires with bare ends or, even better, wires with alligator clips*

From Activity 9, you can see why the diaphragm in a telephone vibrates when you speak into the mouthpiece. In this activity, you'll investigate Edison's discovery that the resistance of carbon changes with pressure. You can do that by seeing how the electric current changes when you vary the pressure on some carbon. You'll need a current detector—a simple galvanoscope that you can build from a magnetic compass and a long piece of enameled copper wire will do.

Cut a piece of the wire about 4.5 m (5 yd) long and wind it into a coil by wrapping it around the compass, as shown in Figure 12. Be sure to wind all the wire in the same direction. Leave about 30 cm (1 ft) of uncoiled wire at each end. Wrap a small piece of masking tape around each side of the coil to keep the wires in place. Use sandpaper to remove about 2.5 cm (1 in.) of the insulation (enamel) from each end of the wire.

To see that your galvanoscope does detect electric current, use a little clay to hold the coil and compass in place (see Figure 13). Be sure the wires in the coil are parallel with the compass needle. Tap the compass gently to free the needle. What happens to the compass needle when you connect the bare ends of the two leads from the coil to opposite poles of a D–cell? (**Don't connect the coil to the D–cell for long or you'll wear down the cell.**)

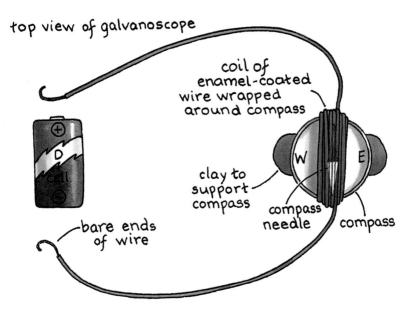

top view of galvanoscope

coil of enamel-coated wire wrapped around compass

clay to support compass

bare ends of wire

compass needle

compass

Figure 12. A galvanoscope can be made from a magnetic compass and a coil of wire.

Set up the electric circuit shown in Figure 13. If you don't have wires with alligator clips, you can bear the ends of the enameled wires with sandpaper and tape them to the roofing nail and spoon. The roofing nail will be used to apply pressure to the graphite (carbon). Put something under the spoon's handle to keep it level and tape it in place. Place some graphite on the spoon. The graphite, which is finely divided carbon, is similar to the carbon granules used in telephones.

Watch the galvanoscope as you gently touch the graphite with the head of the nail. Does the galvanoscope indicate a current? What happens to the current as you very gently increase the pressure on the graphite? Does the electrical resistance of carbon increase or decrease with pressure? Ask an adult to help you dispose of the graphite.

Fax It

Fax it! has become a common phrase in the business community. Transmission of words and images by facsimile, which means "to make the same," has become very popular in recent years, but it has existed since the 1920s. The document to be faxed is scanned by a detector sensitive to the light reflected from the pages. The signal's strength, which depends on the amount of light received by the detector, is converted to an electric current, amplified, and converted to sound before entering the telephone line.

At the other end of the line, the sound is converted to electrical signals that are inverted so that large currents, produced where the light was intense, become small currents and vice versa. The signals travel along a stylus that makes contact with heat-sensitive paper on a drum. The electric current in the stylus heats the paper, which contains carbon. Where the current is large, more carbon is "burned," making the paper darker. Smaller currents produce grayish areas. When the current is zero, the paper remains white.

It was 1888 when Heinrich Hertz (1857–1894) discovered that

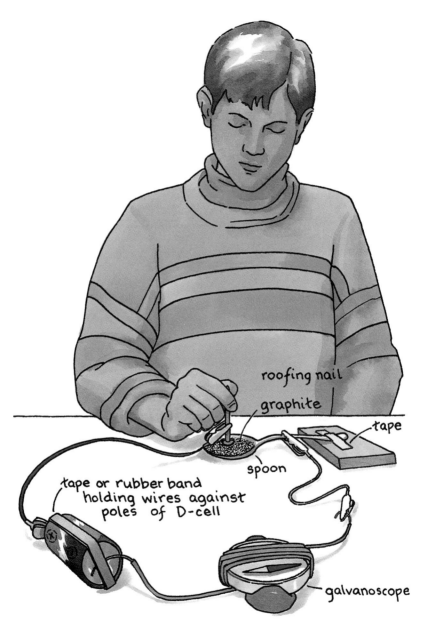

roofing nail

graphite

tape

spoon

tape or rubber band
holding wires against
poles of D-cell

galvanoscope

Figure 13. This is a circuit designed to test the effect of pressure on the resistance of carbon particles.

many kinds of metal plates, if charged negatively, readily discharge when exposed to ultraviolet light—the invisible light that tans your skin and can cause skin cancer. He went on to find that negatively charged metals such as sodium, potassium, and cesium could be discharged by visible light as well as ultraviolet light.

As you read above, a fax machine converts light to an electric current. Producing a flow of electric charge from light is known as the photoelectric effect. Here, then, is another example of how a scientific discovery was later used in a new technology.

ACTIVITY 11

PHOTOELECTRICITY: LIGHT TO ELECTRICITY

MATERIALS
- *small-wattage night-light that goes on automatically in dim light*
- *red lightbulb and lamp*
- *infrared lightbulb and lamp*

Photoelectric devices used to consist of metallic surfaces mounted in a vacuum tube. Today, solid-state photocells have replaced vacuum tubes, but the principle is the same.

Many devices such as the automatic door openers found in supermarkets and security systems that detect burglars use a beam of ultraviolet light that shines on a photocell, producing a current. The current operates an electromagnet that attracts a switch, keeping another circuit open. If someone crosses the beam, the photoelectric current is shut off. This turns off the electromagnet and the switch it controls closes, allowing a current to flow that opens the door or sets off an alarm.

Some small-wattage night-lights are controlled by a photoelectric current. As darkness falls, the light goes on automatically. If you examine such a light, you'll find a light-sensitive area on the side opposite the plug. What happens when you shade the light-sensitive area with your hand? How can you make the light turn on? Will the light go off if you shine red light on it? Shine an infrared light on the light-sensitive area. Does the light go off? Do you think the energy of light is related to its color?

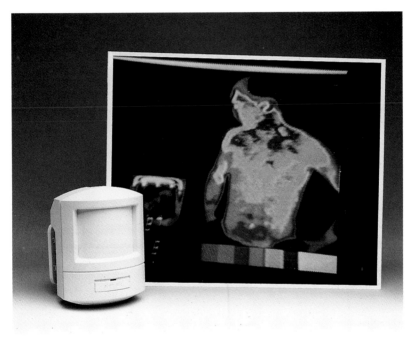

An infrared detector used in security systems

3

COMMUNICATION
BY WAVES

In 1856, James Clerk Maxwell (1831–1879) predicted the existence of electromagnetic waves. Using mathematics and physics, Maxwell theorized that whenever electric charges speed up or slow down, they generate waves that travel through space at the speed of light. These waves consist of an oscillating electric field (a field that is constantly changing from one direction to the opposite). He reasoned that the oscillating electric field would be accompanied by a magnetic field that would oscillate at the same rate. Because the waves are made up of oscillating electric *and* magnetic fields, they became known as electromagnetic waves. We can't see these waves, but Figure 14 shows one way to represent them.

As you may know, a magnetic field gives the direction and strength of the magnetic force on the pole of a magnet or a coil that acts like a magnet. The direction of the field is the direction the north-seeking pole of a compass needle points. The strength of the field is the force exerted on another magnetic pole and is shown by the concentration of the lines of force. Where the lines are close together, the field is strong. An electric field is similar to a magnetic field, but it gives the direction and strength of the electric force on a charged particle at any given point in space.

It was Heinrich Hertz, of photoelectric fame, who first demonstrated that electromagnetic waves could be produced in a form we

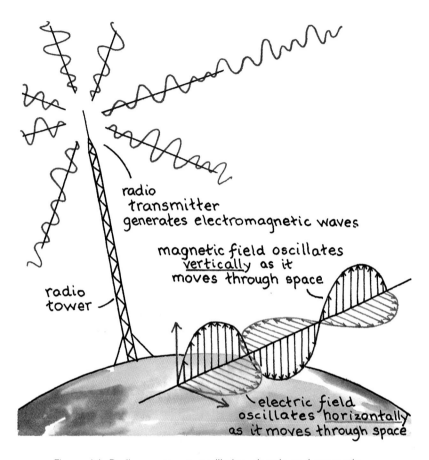

radio
transmitter
generates electromagnetic waves

magnetic field oscillates
vertically as it
moves through space

radio
tower

electric field
oscillates horizontally
as it moves through space

Figure 14. Radio waves are oscillating electric and magnetic fields that constitute an electromagnetic wave. All such waves travel through space at the speed of light—300,000 km/s (186,000 mi/s).

call radio waves today. Hertz found these waves are produced whenever electric charges change their velocity. Within a decade after Hertz's discovery, Guglielmo Marconi (1874–1937) used radio waves to send messages. Marconi's system of communication required no wires to carry impulses, which is why it was called wireless telegraphy. In the next activity, you will produce radio waves in the same way that Hertz did. For convenience, however, you'll use a radio to detect the waves (static).

MAKING AND RECEIVING RADIO WAVES

MATERIALS
- *wire strippers*
- *piece of plastic-coated (insulated) copper wire about 10 to 12 cm (4 to 5 in.) long*
- *6-volt dry-cell battery*
- *small battery-powered radio*
- *aluminum foil large enough to completely cover radio*

Use wire strippers to remove about an inch of insulation from both ends of the piece of insulated wire. Attach one end of the wire to one pole of the 6-volt battery. Turn on the small battery-powered radio. Tune the radio so that it is between stations and all you hear is some mild static. Now touch the free end of the wire to the other pole of the battery. A small spark will be produced as electrons jump between the wire and the battery pole. These accelerating electrons should produce radio waves. Listen carefully! Can you detect radio waves on the small radio when you touch the bare end of the wire to the battery pole?

Cover the radio completely by wrapping it in a sheet of aluminum foil. Again, generate radio waves by touching the bare end of the wire to the pole of the battery. Can you detect any radio waves on the small radio when it is covered with metal? Can you explain the effect of the metal foil?

Hertz and Radio Waves

According to Maxwell's theory, all electromagnetic waves, which include light waves, would travel through space at the speed of light—300,000 km/s (186,000 mi/s). Maxwell made no attempt to demonstrate how such waves might be produced or detected. As so often happens in science, he left the practical aspects of his theory and the technological possibilities to others.

In 1888, Heinrich Hertz made a radio-wave transmitter by connecting two movable metal spheres (S_1 and S_2 in Figure 15) on rods to a large coil of wire. By connecting the coil to a battery, Hertz could make sparks (charges) jump across the gap between the two rods just as you did when you touched a wire to the pole of a battery. By moving the spheres closer together or farther apart, he could change the rate at which the charges jumped across the gap.

According to Maxwell, the charges, which speed up as they move between the two spheres, should produce an electric field. This oscillating field would move through space until it reached a

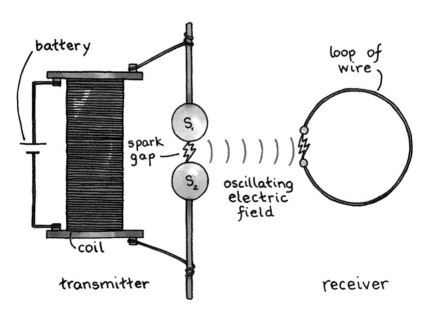

Figure 15. Hertz generated electromagnetic waves on a simple transmitter like the one shown here. When properly tuned, the waves could produce a signal on a receiver some distance away. With today's radios, the listener tunes the receiver to the frequency of the broadcasting station.

conductor where it would push charges (electrons) back and forth. To detect the oscillating electric field in the electromagnetic waves, Hertz placed a loop of wire with a single spark gap a few feet away from his transmitter. He reasoned that when the field reached the loop, it would push charges within the wire back and forth. By adjusting the distance between the spheres in his transmitter, he was able to match the rate of oscillation of the charges in his receiver with those in his transmitter. When sparks began jumping back and forth across the gap in the receiver, he knew the rates matched. Later, Hertz was able to detect these same waves at distances of several hundred feet.

You used a radio to detect the electric field. Instead of adjusting the sparks produced at the transmitter (battery), you tuned the radio to receive the waves produced; that is, you adjusted the radio so that charges in its receiving circuit oscillated at the same rate as those in the sparks produced at the battery.

To demonstrate the wavelike nature of these signals, which could be transmitted through space and detected, Hertz showed that his radio waves could be reflected, refracted (bent), and absorbed just like light. In your experiment, you absorbed the waves by covering the receiver (radio) with aluminum foil. The energy in the electric field was used to move charges back and forth in the aluminum. By the time the field passed through the metal, it had given up most of its energy and so had little effect on the radio. You may notice the same thing on a car radio when you drive across a bridge that consists of metal girders that surround the road.

RESONANCE

MATERIALS
- *book*
- *string*
- *coat hanger*
- *metal washers*
- *clock or watch with second hand*

The oscillating frequency of the charges in Hertz's receiver, like the rate of oscillation of a pendulum, had a natural frequency. To detect the transmitted frequency, Hertz needed a receiver with a matching natural frequency. In your experiment, you matched the frequencies by tuning the radio. The dial found on a radio is used to adjust the receiver so that its charges oscillate with a frequency that matches the frequency of the waves transmitted by the broadcasting station to which you wish to listen.

Matching frequencies is quite common. If a note played on a violin has the same frequency as a particular piano string, the piano string will begin to oscillate when sound waves from the violin reach it. This effect is called resonance.

To demonstrate resonance, hang a book from a string, as shown in Figure 16a. Pull the book a short distance to one side and release it. What is the suspended book's natural frequency of oscillation? That is, how many times does it make one complete swing (over and back) in one minute?

Stop the book and try to set it back into motion by blowing on it. At what frequency should you blow on the book to make it oscillate back and forth again? At what other frequencies can you blow on the book and make it oscillate?

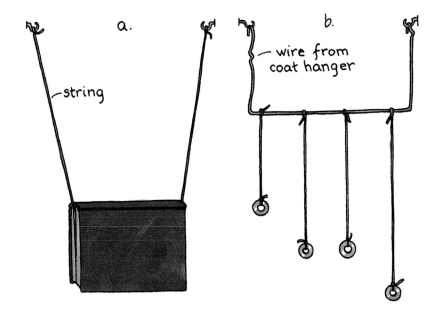

Figure 16: a. What is the book's natural frequency of oscillation? b. What is the natural frequency of each of the pendulums? Do any two have the same natural frequency?

If you change the length of the string from which the book is suspended, how does it affect the book's natural rate of swinging?

Open a coat hanger and use it to suspend four pendulums, as shown in Figure 16b. The pendulums are made from identical metal washers attached to lengths of thread. Notice that two of the pendulums have the same length. A third is longer than the equal-length pendulums and a fourth is shorter than the others. Pull one of the two equal-length pendulums slightly to one side and let it go. Do you think any of the other three pendulums will begin to oscillate? If so, which one do you think it will be? Were you right?

Can you make the longest pendulum oscillate at its natural

frequency by moving the wire from which the pendulums are suspended back and forth at a particular rate? Can you make the shortest pendulum oscillate in the same way?

Marconi and Wireless Communication

In 1894, after reading about Hertz's work, Marconi believed he could use Hertzian waves as a means of communication. His experiments revealed that he could indeed transmit messages over large distances with these waves. But to do so required a more powerful transmitter, a long wire stretching high into the air to serve as an antenna, and a more effective receiver.

In 1899, Marconi sent wireless messages across the English Channel. By 1901, he was successful in sending signals across the Atlantic Ocean. Soon after, Reginald Fessenden (1866–1932) found that he could modulate the regular frequency waves sent by a wireless transmitter; that is, he could use sound waves to vary the amplitude of the regular (carrier) waves transmitted by wireless, as shown in Figure 17. At a receiver, these variations could be sorted out and reconverted back to sound. In 1906, the first modulated radio wave was transmitted and receivers were able to pick up music.

Although 1906 might be considered as the birth date of radio, it was 1920 before the first radio station was established in Pittsburgh. Two years later, there were 600 stations and more than a million listeners!

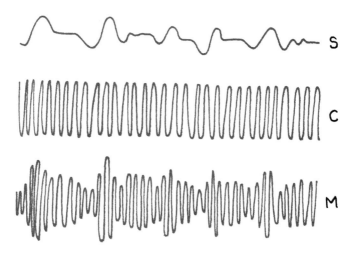

Figure 17. Fessenden found he could use sound waves S to modulate the constant frequency carrier waves C. The modulated waves M were then transmitted through space. The modulation shown here is amplitude (wave height) modulation (AM). It is also possible to modulate the carrier wave's frequency (FM).

WATER WAVES AS A MODEL OF RADIO WAVES

MATERIALS
- *sink or basin*
- *water*
- *cork or similar small floating object*
- *eyedropper (optional)*
- *wooden dowel or candle*
- *large jar*

As you know, radio waves travel through space as oscillating electric and magnetic fields. In fact, all electromagnetic waves (see Figure 18) travel in the same way at the same speed. Although expensive equipment is required to generate most

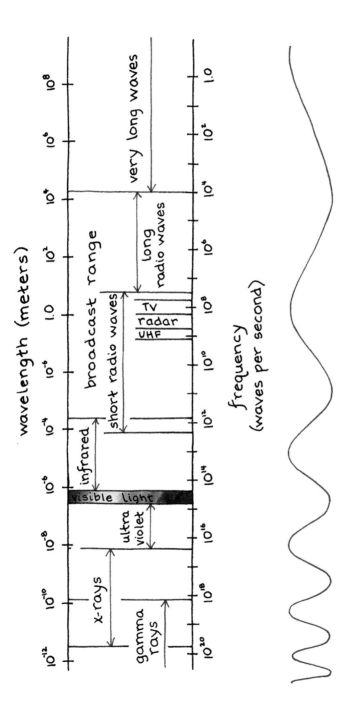

Figure 18. Electromagnetic waves come in a great variety of wavelengths and frequencies. Values for wavelength (top) and frequency (bottom) in the diagram are given in powers of ten. For example, 10^3 means 1,000. The exponent 3 gives the number of zeros after the 1. For negative exponents such as -3 in 10^{-3} or 0.001, the -3 shows that the 1 is 3 places to the right of the decimal point. What happens to the wavelength as the frequency increases?

electromagnetic waves, water waves can serve as a useful model for other kinds of waves.

Fill a large sink or basin with water to a depth of several inches. If you dip your finger into the water, you can see a circular wave (or waves) spread outward across the water's surface. This is the way radio waves, at a much greater speed, move outward from an antenna. A shadow of the wave can be seen on the bottom of the sink. You'll see the wave reflect back from the sides of the sink just as light reflects from a mirror.

Place a cork or some other small object that floats on the water. Notice that the cork bobs up and then down when a wave passes; it does not move with the wave. It is the wave that moves; the water moves mostly up and down.

Hold a wooden dowel or candle upright in the water, with its base on the bottom of the sink. Use the index finger on your other hand to produce waves, one after the other. Notice how the waves go around the candle. Waves with a long wavelength go around objects smaller than their wavelength as if they weren't even there. We say the waves diffract around the objects.

Replace the dowel or candle with a large jar. You'll find that the waves no longer go all the way around the jar. Waves striking an object that is large relative to the wavelengths striking them do not diffract around the object completely. Radio waves are not obstructed by most buildings because the waves are longer than the buildings. As a result, they diffract around the structures.

Improving Radio

Marconi's wireless led to radio, and radio has improved significantly during the century in which it has existed. The electrical circuits used to send and detect radio waves are much more sophisticated than the ones used by Hertz or Marconi. Shortly after wireless communication began, J. A. Fleming (1849–1945) developed the diode. His device, shown in Figure 19a, was based on the Edison Effect, first discovered by Thomas Edison in his search for a satisfactory electric lightbulb. When a metal cylinder (cathode) inside a vacuum tube is heated, an electric current will cross the vacuum to a positively charged plate (called the anode). The current will not cross the vacuum if the plate is negatively charged.

After the discovery of the electron, it was clear that the particles moving across the vacuum were electrons. Because electrons carry a negative charge, they will be attracted to the anode only if it is charged positively. Since charge can flow only one way across a diode, diodes can be used to convert an alternating current to a direct current. An alternating current is one that flows back and forth, such as the electricity in your home. Batteries, on the other hand, provide direct current. The electrons travel from the battery's negative terminal toward its positive terminal.

Lee De Forest (1873–1961) soon modified Fleming's diode to make a triode (see Figure 19b) by placing a grid between the cathode and the anode. The grid was made of wires that could be charged, but the wires were so thin that they did not interfere with electrons passing through the grid to the anode.

A triode can be used to amplify electrical signals; for example, the varying current in a telephone circuit can be connected to the cathode and grid of the triode. The current passing through the grid will reflect the current variations in the telephone wire. By putting more positive charge on the anode, the current coming through the grid can be increased (amplified), thus enhancing the current variations without changing the nature of the variations that would eventually reach the receiver (see Figure 20).

Vacuum tube diodes and triodes (even tetrodes and pentodes) were used to improve radio signals. Later, the tubes were used in television and computers. Such tubes required a lot of power, they got hot, and eventually they would fail. Following World War II, William Shockley, John Bardeen, and Walter Brattain, working at

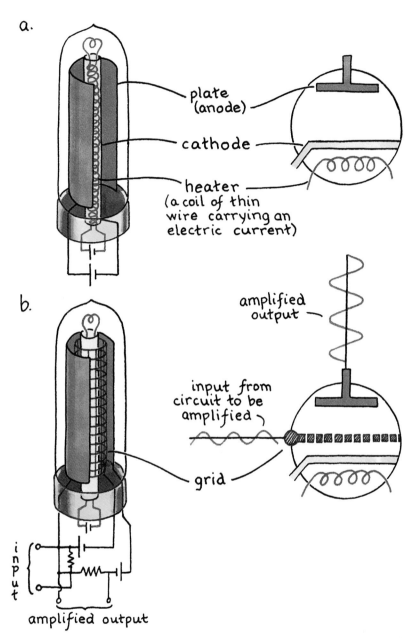

a.

plate (anode)

cathode

heater (a coil of thin wire carrying an electric current)

b.

amplified output

input from circuit to be amplified

grid

input

amplified output

Figure 19: a. When the cathode of a diode is heated, electrons (e⁻) "boil" off its surface. If the anode is positively charged (see connection to battery), electrons will move from cathode to anode across the vacuum. If the anode is negatively charged, fewer or no electrons will get across. b. A triode has a grid between the cathode and anode. The grid makes it possible to amplify (increase) a current.

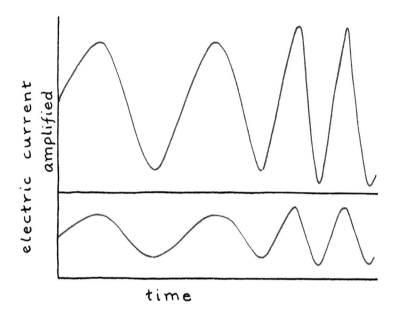

Figure 20. The lower graph shows the fluctuations in an electric current over a period of time. The upper graph shows the result of amplifying the current. The size (amplitude) of the fluctuations are about three times greater during the same periods of time.

Bell Laboratories, found that they could use crystals to replace the work done by vacuum tubes. By adding impurities such as arsenic or antimony to silicon—a process known as doping—they were able to make what are called *n*-type semiconductors. Doping silicon with atoms of aluminum, boron, or gallium led to *p*-type semiconductors. The designation *p* or *n* refers to the way charge is transmitted in the crystal. In an *n*-type crystal, charge is carried by electrons; in a *p*-type crystal, charge is carried by what are called holes—the absence of electrons, which is the equivalent of positive charge.

Today, semiconductors have replaced vacuum tubes in most

electronic devices. As Figure 21 shows, diodes and triodes can be made from *p*- and *n*-type semiconductors. Because these devices are small and can be easily joined on tiny silicon chips, integrated circuits containing hundreds of individual circuits are now made for various electronic devices. Computers, which once filled a large room with vacuum tubes and wires, can now be carried about in a small case. Furthermore, semiconductors require no warm-up time, use little power, and seldom fail. Their light weight and small size have enabled manufacturers to produce miniaturized versions of almost everything—TV cameras and receivers, radios, watches, calculators, computers, and so on.

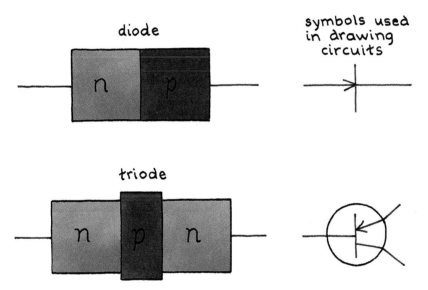

Figure 21. Diodes and triodes can be made from *p*- and *n*-type semiconductors.

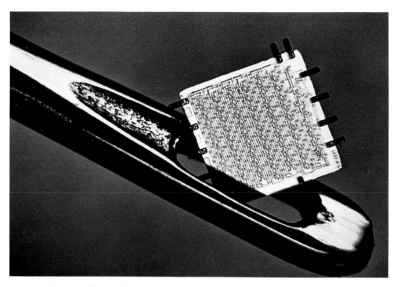

A tiny silicon chip can fit easily into the eye of a needle.

The Science and Technology Leading to Television

Television signals travel through space in the same way that radio signals do. The only difference is the wavelength, as you saw in Figure 18. But generating and receiving TV signals is a different matter because light as well as sound must be used to modulate the carrier wave.

The TV set in your home is based on discoveries made around 1900. Prior to that time, great strides had been achieved in the technology of making vacuum tubes and producing high-voltage electricity (the equivalent of thousands of flashlight cells connected end to end), which provides electric charges with lots of energy. It was found that when high voltage is applied across a vacuum tube, as shown in Figure 22a, a greenish glow appears at the end of the tube opposite the negative electrode (cathode). A metal plate supported in the middle of the tube will produce a shadow in the glow, indicating that the rays come from the cathode, which is why they were called cathode rays.

Were these rays light waves or charged particles? Further experiments showed that magnetic fields caused the rays to bend in the way moving negatively charged particles would be expected to bend (see Figure 22b). By building a tube that enclosed parallel metal plates that could be oppositely charged, Sir J. J. Thomson (1856–1940) confirmed that the rays were negatively charged particles (see Figure 22c). Thomson went on to show that the particles, which came to be known as electrons, were the fundamental units of negative charge found in the atoms of all matter.

The combined work of Thomson, Fleming, and De Forest led to the development of the cathode ray oscilloscope shown in Figure 23a. The electron gun at the rear of the tube produces a beam of electrons that accelerate as they are pulled toward the anode. Unless some force acts on the electrons coming through the hole in the anode, they will continue on until they strike a fluorescent screen, where a visible dot of light indicates their presence. By charging the horizontal plates, the electron beam can be bent up or down. A similar pair of vertical plates can be used to bend the electron beam to the right or left.

The charge on the vertical plates can be changed in such a way that the electron beam is swept across the screen at a steady speed and then quickly returned to its initial position at the left of the screen (as you view it). If the horizontal plates are connected to a source of varying voltage that changes the amount and even the sign (+ or -) of the charge on the plates, the electron beam can be made to move up and down as it moves from left to right across the screen. For example, Figure 23b shows the pattern seen when the horizontal plates are connected to a household circuit where the voltage varies from +170 volts to -170 volts and back to +170 volts every 1/60 second.

The television set in your home is very similar to the oscilloscope described above. However, the electrons used to create TV images are deflected not by charged plates but by magnetic fields produced by electric currents in coils of wire.

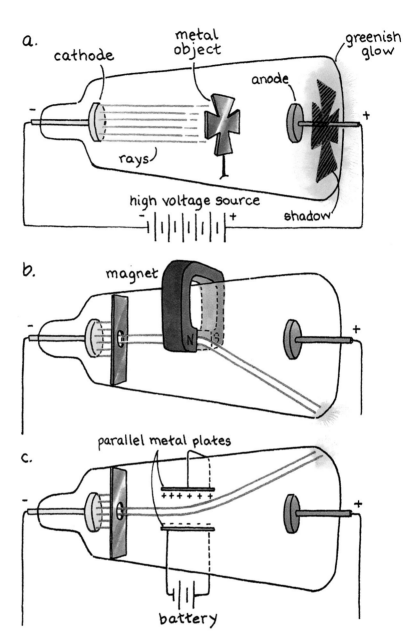

Figure 22: a. Cathode rays produce a greenish glow when they strike glass in an evacuated tube. b. The bending of the rays by a magnetic field indicated that the rays were negatively charged particles. c. Bending the rays with an electric field inside the tube confirmed that the rays were negatively charged particles.

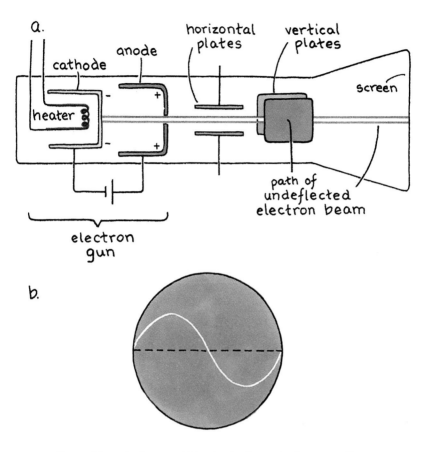

Figure 23: a. A diagram (side view) of a cathode ray oscilloscope reveals the path of the electron beam. b. This shows an
oscilloscope screen when the vertical plates sweep the beam
across the screen every 1/60 second and the horizontal plates
are connected to a household circuit. The dotted line shows
the pattern when the horizontal plates are disconnected.

ACTIVITY 15

A MODEL OF AN ELECTRON IN A MAGNETIC FIELD

MATERIALS
- *small steel ball (marble size)*
- *grooved ruler*

- *washers or small piece of wood to place under one end of ruler*
- *smooth, flat tabletop*
- *ceramic magnets—ring, disk, or rectangular*

Electrons emerging from the electron gun at the back of a television's cathode ray tube are bent as they pass through magnetic fields produced by currents in coils of wire. You can make a simple model of this effect using a steel ball to represent an electron and ceramic magnets to provide a magnetic field.

Let a steel ball roll down a grooved ruler, one end of which is raised about half an inch. The ball represents an electron. Note the path of the ball as it rolls along a level table. Place a ceramic magnet near the ball's path, as shown in Figure 24. Place it close enough to the path so that it affects the ball but not so close that it "grabs" it. What happens to the ball as it rolls through the magnetic field?

ACTIVITY 16

A MAGNET'S EFFECT ON BLACK-AND-WHITE TV

MATERIALS
- *black-and-white TV set (**Do not use a color television. The color mask in a color set contains iron that can be magnetized, producing permanent distortions in the picture.**)*
- *strong magnet*

From what you have learned, what do you think will happen if you hold a magnet near a black-and-white TV screen? To find out, hold the magnet at various positions around and on the front of the screen. What effect does it have? Was your predic-

68

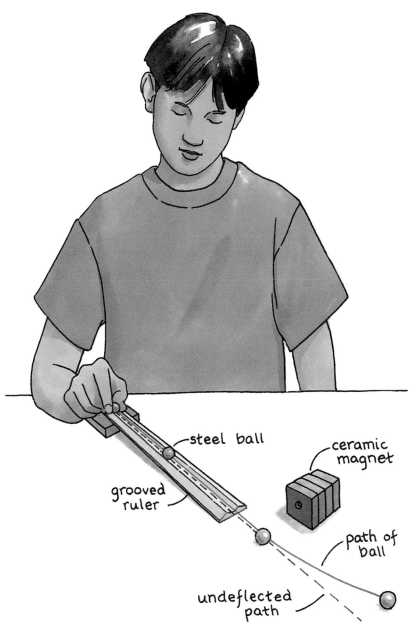

steel ball

ceramic magnet

grooved ruler

path of ball

undeflected path

Figure 24. A steel ball and a magnet can be used to make a model of the way electrons in a television set are affected by a magnetic field.

tion correct? What is the effect of reversing the magnet; that is, holding the south, as opposed to the north, pole near the set?

A TV Picture

As you've read, a TV set contains an electron gun with deflecting coils that can direct the electron beam to various positions on the screen. To make a picture on the screen, the beam sweeps across the screen 525 times in 1/30 second, striking some 460 phosphor dots in each line—a total of nearly 250,000 dots for each image. For black-and-white TV, information about brightness on the carrier wave is demodulated (changed from an electromagnetic wave back to electrical impulses) and used to turn the electron beam on or off. At spots on the screen where electrons strike, the phosphors emit light; other areas remain dark.

In color sets, three electron guns are used. Each beam is aimed at one of three different types of phosphors on the screen. One type emits red light, another emits green light, and a third emits blue light. As you know, combinations of these three primary colors can create all the colors in the rainbow. Of course, the phosphors chosen emit light for only a short time, so the picture keeps changing so fast that we don't notice it.

TV From the Camera's End

The source of the images you see on a TV screen is a TV camera. Light passing through the camera's lens strikes a photosensitive surface, causing the release of electrons. Where the light is intense, many electrons are released; dim light produces fewer electrons. The electrons provide an electrically charged pattern that is scanned and used to modulate the carrier wave.

In the case of color television, the image is separated into three colored images (red, green, and blue) by semitransparent mirrors that selectively reflect different colors, as shown in Figure 25. Such mirrors are only partially silvered so that only a portion of the light is reflected and the rest is transmitted. Additional filters in front of three scanning tubes allow separate electrical signals to be created for red, green, and blue light.

Because the TV signals transmitted are received by both color and black-and-white sets, both a brightness and a color signal must be used to modulate the carrier wave. The signals from the three color tubes are mixed to produce a brightness signal for each part of the image. These same three signals are also combined in a color encoder that allows the amounts of color in each part of the image to be modulated separately. Finally, a sound signal is added to the carrier wave before transmission. At the receiving end, a black-and-white set will respond to the brightness but not the color signal.

Modern television cameras can be moved with ease to cover events in various places.

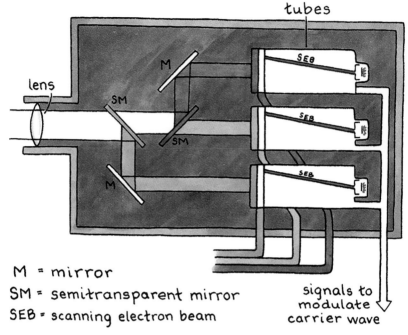

tubes

lens

M = mirror
SM = semitransparent mirror
SEB = scanning electron beam

signals to
modulate
carrier wave

Figure 25. A camera for color TV produces three images—
red, green, and blue. Each image is scanned to obtain an electrical signal used to modulate the carrier wave.

ACTIVITY 17

A CLOSE LOOK AT A COLOR TV SCREEN

MATERIALS
- *strong magnifying glass*
- *ruler*
- *color TV set*

With a strong magnifying glass you can see the tiny bars on a
TV screen that produce color. Make an estimate of the size of
the bars and the total number on the screen. If possible, look
at a solid patch of red, blue, or green on the screen. Are all the

bars releasing color? What happens when the color changes? How are the three types of phosphors able to produce other colors such as yellow and magenta?

Storing Information

Not only can we enjoy the images created by television; we can store these images for future use by recording the TV signals on videotape. Similarly, computer data can be stored on diskettes. Both storage mechanisms are based on the magnetic fields produced by electric currents. Figure 26 shows how a video head spins as the magnetic tape moves by it. Diagonal magnetic tracks are produced on the tape. Once the signals have been recorded on the tape, they can serve as signals for a TV receiver.

More recently, compact discs are being used to store information. The discs, like computers, use a digital system of ones and zeros. A disc contains a spiral pattern of pits (zeros) and unpitted surface (ones). As it spins, a laser beam scans the disc. No light is reflected from pits so no electrical signal is produced. This corresponds to a zero. The unpitted track surface reflects light producing an electrical signal (a one) that can be accepted by a variety of receivers.

ACTIVITY 18

MAGNETIC TAPE

MATERIALS
- *iron filings or fine steel wool, scissors, and paper*
- *white paper*
- *sheet of cardboard about 30 cm (1 ft) on a side*
- *a strong permanent magnet*
- *electromagnet (optional)*

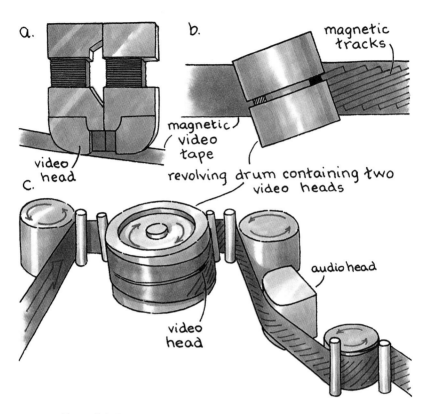

a.

b.

magnetic tracks

magnetic
video
tape

video
head

c.

revolving drum containing two
video heads

audio head

video
head

Figure 26. Electrical signals are changed to magnetic patterns on videotape. The patterns can be converted back to electrical signals to produce pictures and sound on a TV receiver. a. Inside the video head, electric coils create a varying magnetic pattern. b. A spinning drum containing two heads transfers the magnetic patterns to a tape, guided by rollers, that passes over the drum. To put as much information in as little space as possible, the magnetic tracks are laid down in diagonal fashion across the tape. c. An audio head produces a soundtrack as a separate magnetic band on one side of the tape.

Never put diskettes or magnetic tapes near a magnet. The reason is that they are coated with a magnetic film. The film, generally made of plastic, contains patterns made from magnetic particles within the plastic. A magnet can change the patterns that may be on the film.

With iron filings and a magnet, you can see the principle involved in establishing such patterns on tape. Obtain some iron filings from your school science teacher, a hobby shop, or make them from steel wool. To make them, you'll need a new pad of fine steel wool. Find the end of the roll and unroll it a few inches. To eliminate stray long fibers, trim the end and sides of the roll with scissors. Then using the scissors, cut very narrow strips from the roll. Make the strips as narrow as you can so that the fibers will be very short. Let the tiny pieces of steel fall onto a sheet of paper. You can then use the sheet as a chute to empty the particles into an old salt or pepper shaker.

Sprinkle some of the iron filings on a piece of white paper that you have taped to a sheet of cardboard, as shown in Figure 27. What happens to the filings when you hold a magnet underneath and close to the cardboard? What happens when you move the magnet and when you rotate it? What can you do to change the pattern you see in the iron filings? Can you produce a pattern by pulling the cardboard over a stationary magnet? What happens when you turn the cardboard above such a magnet?

When information is encoded on a magnetic tape or disc, it is done with small coils of wire carrying an electric current that varies in strength. The process can be reversed by moving the tape with its magnetic patterns beneath a head that contains small coils of wire. The changing magnetic patterns (magnetic fields) produce small electric currents in the coil. When amplified, these currents serve as signals that activate other electrical patterns in a computer, pictures on a television screen, sound on a tape player, and so on.

Use the electromagnet you made in Activity 8 in place of the permanent magnet and repeat this experiment. How can you change the strength of the electromagnet? How does changing the magnet's strength affect the pattern seen in the iron filings?

Figure 27. What happens to the iron filings when you move a magnet under the cardboard?

4

COMMUNICATION
IN THE FUTURE

Since World War II, a number of discoveries, inventions, and engineering developments have had a significant impact on communication technology throughout the world. In 1959, the first integrated circuit was patented. This device, often referred to as a chip, consists of a tiny piece of semiconducting material, usually silicon, with built-in solid-state diodes, triodes, and transistors (devices that can amplify or change electric currents). Chips containing integrated circuits have become smaller and smaller—a development that has led to desktop computers that have the capacity to store huge amounts of information within a very small space.

You have already seen how a beam from a laser, which was invented in 1960, is used to retrieve information from compact discs. The laser can also be used with optical fibers—thin strands of glass or plastic—to transmit messages in the form of light pulses. The light, which stays within the fibers, is transmitted at the speed of light in glass, which is 200,000 km/s (124,000 mi/s), over large distances without need for amplification. Information transmitted as electrical pulses along copper wires must be amplified every 600 m (2,000 ft).

Three years before the invention of the laser, *Sputnik I*, the first artificial satellite, was launched by the Soviet Union and went into orbit about the earth. Since that time, a large number of satellites have been placed in space, and many of them are still in orbit. Some of these satellites are used for communication. They reflect radio and TV waves so that information in the form of sounds, text, and images can be conveyed around the world almost instantaneously. Satellites also communicate information about the earth's weather, forests, and oceans, as well as classified data about foreign military sites. For example, satellite cameras can detect changes in the ocean's color that indicate the concentration of tiny phytoplankton on which other sea-dwelling organisms depend for food.

A series of satellites in orbit about the earth's poles at altitudes of more than 16,000 km (10,000 mi) make up the NAVSTAR global positioning system (GPS). These satellites transmit radio signals that can be picked up by ships at sea. The signals are sent at very precise moments in time. By comparing the time the signal was sent with the time it is received by the ship, the distance of the ship from the satellite can be established. By using three or more such signals, a ship's position can be determined to within a few meters. The calculations are done quickly by a computer connected to the receiver and the latitude and longitude are then displayed on a screen.

In the future, automobiles may be connected to a similar system. Signals from satellites will be used to map a car's position. That position will then appear on a map found on a computer monitor mounted on the car's dashboard. A driver could use the map to return to a sought-after route or to find a less-traveled route during rush-hour traffic.

The past decade has seen the rapid growth of wireless cellular mobile telephones. You have probably seen someone using such a phone in his or her automobile. The word *cellular* refers to the fact that an area in which such a telephone is used is divided into cells. Each cell has a radio transmitter and receiver that is used to relay signals from the caller's phone to the phone where the call is being received. If a cellular telephone moves from one cell to another during a conversation, a computer transfers the signal from one transmitter and receiver to another without interrupting the conversation.

The Information Superhighway

The technologies discussed above are now being combined with television (a postwar development that we now take for granted) and telephones to produce what many are calling the information superhighway.

In less than a decade, the combination of telephone and television (videophones) that makes it possible to see the person at the other end of the line may become widespread. Several decades from now, it's likely that the telephone will emerge as our personal link to a worldwide communication, entertainment, and information network. Everyone will probably carry his or her own Dick Tracy-type miniaturized telephone. Telephones and telephone numbers

Videophones are becoming a part of a worldwide communications network.

will become a personal item so that anyone can be reached at any time. To provide privacy, miniaturized answering systems that can access fax machines will be a part of the system.

Eventually, videophones will be united with computers and television to provide a technology that will expand both our information and entertainment menus. A small but powerful computer will be added to the cable TV terminal box found on television sets. The computer will allow you to travel to thousands of sites along the information superhighway. In many libraries, offices, and homes, it is already possible to access the databases in a network of other libraries, universities, businesses, and government by using modems to connect computers to telephone lines. But in the future, the small computer on your television will allow you to obtain information from the largest libraries and universities in the country.

The same computer will let you access 500 channels, view any movie you want to see, play video games with people in other parts of the world, do your shopping and banking at home, purchase airline tickets to anywhere you would like to visit, watch an athletic contest from any of a number of camera angles, and view the exhibits at a variety of museums. Small slots incorporated into the sets will enable you to use credit cards to purchase items on shopping channels or gain access to important events ranging from symphonies to championship prizefights.

The information superhighway will provide all possible combinations of data in the form of sound, text, and images. The world's greatest teachers may be available to interested students; medical specialists will be able to view patients from afar and analyze their symptoms; businesses will hold video conferences, thus eliminating the need to travel farther than the nearest TV set.

A Problem With Wires

The superhighway along which all this communication will take place consists of the fiber-optic cables that can transmit vast amounts of data without frequent amplification. Ideally, a fiber-optic cable would lead to every home. This will happen sometime in the future, but it will be decades before fiber optics will replace the last 600 m (2,000 ft) of copper cables leading to separate homes and terminals. Instead, switching systems will convert light signals carried long distances on optical fibers to electrical impulses that will travel along the last 600 m (2,000 ft) of cable leading to individual dwellings.

Internet

Today, more than 10,000 computer networks involving libraries, schools, businesses, and government are linked together through a system known as Internet. Internet allows its users to exchange electronic mail and messages left on bulletin boards while providing access to a vast amount of information of all kinds.

Although Internet is open to anyone with a computer and modem, it is extremely difficult to navigate the circuitous routes that lead to various pieces of information. Programmers are striving to solve this problem by designing software (Knowbots) that will quickly search Internet and find the particular information sought by a user.

★ **ACTIVITY 19**

A LIGHT PIPE

MATERIALS
- *45-45-90 prism*
- *scissors*
- *heavy black construction paper*
- *white paper*

- *lightbulb and socket*
- *a dark room*
- *optical-fiber light guide or optical fibers and black plastic tape*
- *flashlight and bulb*

Light signals can be carried along optical fibers for long distances because the light is trapped within the glass. Instead of coming through the sides of the glass, it is reflected back into the transparent material.

With a 45-45-90 glass or plastic prism and a narrow beam of light, you can see how light is totally reflected inside glass or plastic. To make a light beam, use scissors to cut a narrow 1-mm (1/16-in.) slit that is about 8 cm (3 in.) high in the center of a 10-cm (4-in.) by 15-cm (6-in.) sheet of heavy black construction paper. Fold the paper and stand it upright next to a sheet of white paper, as shown in Figure 28. When light from a bulb several meters away in an otherwise-dark room passes through the slit, it creates a narrow beam. Turn the long surface (hypotenuse) of the 45-45-90 prism so the beam is perpendicular to it. As you can see, the beam is totally reflected within the prism at both of the shorter surfaces of the prism. It finally emerges through the long surface, traveling in a direction opposite to that at which it entered the prism.

Turn the prism to change the angle at which the entering beam strikes the shorter side of the prism. Estimate the angle at which some light from the beam begins to pass through the surface of the shorter side. Does all the light pass through or is some still reflected back into the glass?

You have seen that light striking a glass surface at certain angles will be totally reflected; no light will pass through the surface. In fact, for any light ray within the glass, if the angle between the light ray and the surface is less than 48°, all the light will be reflected. As a result, light passing into a long glass rod stays within the glass.

To see how light passes along a glass rod, you can buy an

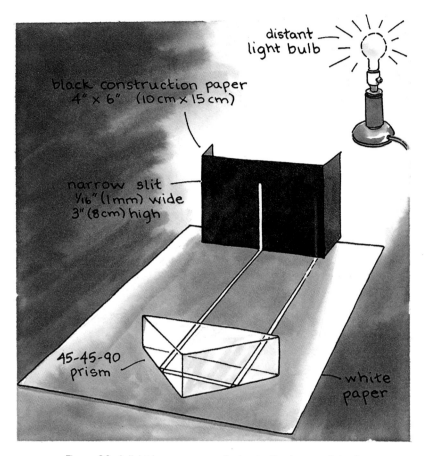

Figure 28. A light beam perpendicular to the long surface (hypotenuse) of a 45-45-90 prism will be reflected twice inside the prism. It will not pass through either of the two shorter surfaces.

optical-fiber light guide in a hobby store or from a scientific supply house, or you might be able to borrow one from your school. If you can't obtain such a light guide, you can make your own by wrapping a long bundle of several dozen thin optical fibers with black plastic tape.

To see how your light guide transmits light, remove the glass cover from the front of a flashlight. Use black construction paper and tape to make a small cylinder that will fit snugly over the flashlight bulb. Place one end of the light guide into the other end of the black paper cylinder so that the guide touches the end of the bulb. When you turn on the flashlight, you can see that light is transmitted along the optical fibers and emerges at the other end of the light guide. Bend the light guide into various shapes. Does light still follow the glass fibers when the guide is bent into various shapes?

Virtual Reality

It is likely that the computelecommunicator sets of the future will connect with head-mounted screens for virtual-reality excursions. Such screens already exist, but they are not yet ready for mass production. A head-mounted screen used for virtual-reality programs is connected to a computer that provides a slightly different image for each of the viewer's eyes. As a result, one sees a three-dimensional view of an environment that can easily be taken to be real.

If the user wears gloves wired with electronic sensors, the computer can measure the movement of the hands and locate them in the virtual space observed by the user. A person wearing the head-mounted screen and wired gloves can pick up, observe, and manipulate the virtual objects in his or her virtual reality. Future plans call for a wired suit that would allow a user to actually enter the space of virtual reality.

Beyond its potential for fun, virtual-reality devices have a variety of practical uses. Medical students wearing a monitor could perform surgery on virtual patients; architects could feed blueprints into a computer and see the completed virtual structure in three dimensions on their head-mounted screens; the educational possibilities are practically infinite.

NASA hopes to use virtual-reality devices to allow astronauts to control the action of robots making repairs outside a spaceship or a space station. Cameras mounted on the robots' heads and wires connected to their hands and body will enable an astronaut inside the ship to actually see and feel through the robot. By moving his or her own hands and body, the astronaut will be able to control the robot and, thereby, carry on construction or make repairs without having to leave the safety provided by the ship.

Home Robots

Although not a part of virtual reality, home computers will be built to respond to light, touch, sound, and even voice signals. These computers will allow you to communicate with robots that will perform many household chores. They will clean your home, answer the door, run a bath, turn on the stove, furnace, or radio, respond to questions as wide ranging as trivia or your finances, and even tell you, if you ask, which movie, newspaper, or virtual-reality excursion you might enjoy at home that evening.

Of course, new discoveries in science may lead to changes in communication that we can't even imagine today. Before the discoveries of Oersted, Michael Faraday (1791–1867), Hertz, and others, no one even dreamed of communicating by telephone, radio, or television. One thing is certain, during your lifetime, the means and mechanisms of communication will change dramatically.

Disabilities, Communication, and Technology

For the disabled, communication is often a problem, but technology has made giant strides in providing systems that allow the blind to read, the deaf to hear, and the paralyzed to write. For the deaf, in addition to sound-amplification systems, there are speech-perception aids that can be worn by the users. One device contains a small computer that analyzes sound for words that are then made visible as print on an eyeglass display. Coupled with lipreading, the device makes it possible for deaf people to perceive ordinary conversation.

For the visually impaired, systems are available that scan print and convert it into vibrating images of the letters that a blind person can feel with his or her fingers. Other systems convert print into spoken words—a technology that dyslexics as well as the visually impaired find helpful. It is even possible to control the rate at which the computer "speaks" so that a visually impaired person can gather information as rapidly as he or she finds comfortable.

Computers that respond to sound and specific words allow quadriplegics not only to control their wheelchairs but to work effectively in a computerized office as well. Once a computer has been turned on by voice, it can be controlled by further spoken commands or by using an infrared head pointer as one might use a mouse on an ordinary computer. The infrared beam can be directed to icons on a screen in the same way that items can be chosen with a mouse. Words can be typed on a keyboard using a mouth-held pencil or stick, and work is under way that will allow spoken words to be converted immediately to print. Systems already exist that will translate text from one language to another.

At Tufts University School of Medicine in Boston, aphasic patients—usually stroke victims who have lost the ability to translate thoughts into words—are learning to organize symbols on a computer to express their ideas. For example, they might use a mouse to move the symbol for a fork to a symbol for food and then move both, in turn, to the face of a cartoon boy to express the idea that the boy is eating.

GOING FURTHER

In this book, you have seen only a small portion of the science and technology involved in communication. There is much more that you can investigate. Some of the things you might like to investigate are listed below.

★ • In what ways has the invention of computers and word-processing programs been a boon to writing?

★ • Investigate various ways of making paper. A few artists still make their own paper by hand. Why would they do this?

★ • Can you find toys that contain magnets? What purpose do the magnets serve? How do the magnets achieve that purpose?

★ • What are the watermarks associated with the paper industry? How and why are they made?

★ • What is Braille? What role does it play in communication? How does it work?

★ • The arrangement of letters on a typewriter keyboard is called the QWERTY system. The reason is obvious if you look at a keyboard. But why were the letters arranged in this manner rather than alphabetically?

★ • In one form of color printing, the material to be color-printed is photographed four times, once with black-and-white film, once through a blue filter, once through a green filter, and once through a red filter. How can these four separate films then be used to print a picture in cyan, magenta, yellow, and black inks?

★ • Together with several friends or classmates, write, print, and publish your own newspaper.

★ • Try communicating with others using Morse code. In how many different ways can you use this code to communicate?

★ • How is a radio tuned so that it receives the "natural" frequency of a particular station?

★ • What is the difference between AM and FM radio? What are the advantages and disadvantages of each one?

★ • Build a small radio of your own. You can find directions for such a task in a variety of books, including *The Thomas Edison Book of Easy and Incredible Experiments,* Wiley, 1988.

✖★ • Under adult supervision, carry out some experiments using a cathode ray oscilloscope.

★ • Visit a radio or TV station.

GLOSSARY

cathode ray oscilloscope: an electron gun at one end of a tube produces a beam of electrons that strike a fluorescent screen at the other end, where a visible dot of light indicates their presence. The beam can be bent up, down, or sideways by an electric field (charged plates) or a magnetic field.

chase: a rectangular frame in which type is held for printing.

cyan: the color formed by mixing blue and green light or by removing red light from white light.

doctor blade: a blade used in gravure printing to clear ink from the space between characters on the printing plate.

Edison Effect: when a metal cylinder (cathode) inside a vacuum tube is heated, an electric current will cross the vacuum to a positively charged plate (called the anode). Current will not cross the vacuum if the plate is negatively charged.

electric field: gives the direction and strength of the electric force near an electric charge. The direction of the field at any point is given by the direction a positive charge would move if placed in the field at that point. The strength of a field may be represented by the concentration of the lines.

electrical resistance: the resistance of an electrical conductor to the flow of charge. The resistance of a conductor is defined as the ratio of the voltage to the current.

electromagnet: wire wound around an iron core that behaves like a magnet when an electric current flows through the wire.

electromagnetic waves: oscillating electric and magnetic fields that travel through space in wavelike fashion at the speed of light.

galvanoscope: a device used to detect an electric current.

gravure: a form of printing in which the characters exist as depressions in a plate. Before paper is pressed against the plate, a doctor blade sweeps across the surface, clearing away ink between the characters.

letterpress: a form of printing in which ink is applied to raised characters. The ink is then transferred to paper when the paper is pressed against the characters.

lithography (photo-offset): a form of printing in which a photograph of the original page is projected onto a thin sheet of zinc or aluminum that has a special chemical coating. A greasy material is deposited on the plate in dark parts of the image. The rest of the plate remains clean and shiny. Water applied to the plate is repelled by the greasy portions of the plate but remains on the shiny parts. When ink is applied, it is repelled by the wet areas but sticks to the grease. The inked image is then transferred from the plate to a rubber-coated cylinder that transfers the ink to paper.

magenta: a purplish-red color made by mixing blue and red light or by removing green light from white light.

magnetic field: gives the direction and strength of the magnetic force around the poles of a magnet or an electromagnet. The direction of the field is the direction the north-seeking pole of a compass needle points. The strength of a field may be represented by the concentration of the lines.

Morse code: a system of communication that uses various combinations of dots and dashes to represent letters and numbers.

papyrus: a kind of paper made by weaving together fibers peeled from reeds.

parchment: dried sheep or goat skin on which words were written.

phosphor: a substance that emits light after absorbing energy from electrons, sunlight, or other radiation.

photoelectric cell: a device that converts light to electricity.

platen: a flat plate used to press paper against the inked type during the printing process.

resonance: when periodic forces applied to an object match the natural period of vibration of the object, that object will begin to vibrate at its natural frequency.

robots: computer-controlled machines that carry out routine tasks.

signature: a large printed sheet made up of four or a multiple of four (usually 16) pages, which, when folded, become a section of a book.

size: a gelatinous substance made from glue, gum, wax, or clay and used as a glaze or filler for porous material such as paper.

tympan: a frame lined with a sheet of felt that was used to hold the paper in position and even out variations in pressure during the printing process.

yellow: the color found when red and green light are mixed together or when blue light is removed from white light.

UNITS AND THEIR ABBREVIATIONS

LENGTH

English	Metric
mile (mi)	kilometer (km)
yard (yd)	meter (m)
foot (ft)	centimeter (cm)
inch (in.)	millimeter (mm)

AREA

English	Metric
square mile (mi^2)	square kilometer (km^2)
square yard (yd^2)	square meter (m^2)
square foot (ft^2)	square centimeter (cm^2)
square inch ($in.^2$)	square millimeter (mm^2)

VOLUME

English	Metric
cubic mile (mi^3)	cubic kilometer (km^3)
cubic yard (yd^3)	cubic meter (m^3)
cubic foot (ft^3)	cubic centimeter (cm^3)
cubic inch ($in.^3$)	cubic millimeter (mm^3)
ounce (oz)	liter (L)
	milliliter (mL)

MASS

English	Metric
pound (lb)	kilogram (kg)
ounce (oz)	gram (g)

TIME

hour (hr)

minute (min)

second (s)

FORCE OR WEIGHT

English	*Metric*
ounce (oz)	newton (N)
pound (lb)	

SPEED OR VELOCITY

English	*Metric*
miles per hour (mi/hr)	kilometers per hour (km/hr)
miles per second (mi/s)	kilometers per second (km/s)
feet per second (ft/s)	meters per second (m/s)
	centimeters per second (cm/s)

TEMPERATURE

English	*Metric*
degrees Fahrenheit (°F)	degrees Celsius (°C)

ENERGY

calorie (cal)

Calorie (Cal)

joule (J)

POWER

watt (W) = joule per second (J/s)

ELECTRICAL UNITS

volt (V)

ampere (A)

MATERIALS

alligator clips
aluminum foil
aluminum frozen-food container, large
balloon
basin or dishpan, large
batteries, D-cell and 6-volt dry cell
black-and-white and color TV sets
blender
boards variety of sizes
book
can
cardboard
ceramic magnets
clay
clock or watch with second hand
coat hanger
cork
curtain, old
diagrams and photographs from books, magazines, or newspapers
drinking glass
eggbeater
electromagnet
enamel-coated copper wire
eyedropper
facial tissues

flashlight
food coloring
45-45-90 prism
glue
graphite
grooved ruler
hammer
ink or ink pad
insulated copper wires
iron, electric household
iron filings or fine steel wool
jar
knife, sharp
laundry starch, instant
lightbulbs (blue, green, red, and infrared)
magnetic compass
magnet, strong
magnifying glass, strong
metal washers
metallic unpainted thumbtacks
microscope
nails
newspaper or blotter paper
night-light
optical fiber light guide

optical fibers
paper—variety of types
paper clips
pencils
pliers
radio
rolling pin
rubber band
ruler
salt
sandpaper
scissors
sink or basin
small steel ball
smooth tabletop

socket
spoons, tablespoon and soup spoon
string
strong light
study lamps
tape, masking and black plastic
tin shears
toothpicks, flat
washers
watercolors and brush
white screen or wall
wire window screen
wire strippers
wooden dowel or candle
wood, various shapes and sizes

INDEX